Chronicles of Destiny

WORKBOOK

Prophetess Tonya McCoy Parker

IN DUE SEASON
Publishing

Chronicles of Destiny
WORKBOOK

Cover Design: Jaylite Publications

Typesetting and Book Layout by
Enger Lanier Taylor for In Due Season Publishing

Published By: In Due Season Publishing
           Huntsville, Alabama 35810
           indueseasonpublishing@gmail.com
           www.indueseasonpublishing@gmail.com

ISBN- 978-0972745628
ISBN- 0972745629

To order additional copies, please contact
Prophetess Tonya McCoy Parker
P.O. Box 3661
Huntsville, AL 35810
Email: Info@TrailblazersIntl.org
Website: www.TrailblazersIntl.org

Chronicles of Destiny Workbook Introduction

From the *Chronicles of Destiny: 40 Days of Devotional Impartation*, we were taught the importance of walking out our purpose and destiny regardless of the circumstances surrounding us or the things that we encounter every day. In the devotional we see how God takes every fiber of our existence and weaves it all together to create something beautiful, full of power, passion, and purpose in Him! It is in this place that He demonstrates to us, how to go from struggles to strength.

Each chronicle confirms that you are on the heart and mind of God and His desire is that you reach the fullness of your capacity while here on earth. There will be problems, but you must be confident that He has also given you people to help solve those problems; a part of your solutions lie within this workbook.

This workbook is designed to expand your awareness, study and development concerning your purpose and destiny in God. It is a place that you do not enter haphazardly, but enter knowing that God has created and designed you with a specific purpose in mind and He will orchestrate your every step in fulfilling what He ordained. However, it is your responsibility to:

Destiny Requires You To...

- ❖ Always give every thought and idea back to Him.
- ❖ Allow Him to shift it and change these ideas as He desires.
- ❖ Commit to studying the Word of God concerning your purpose and destiny.
- ❖ Seek out training and development opportunities to enhance what He has given you to accomplish.
- ❖ Challenge yourself daily to grow in your purpose and destiny.
- ❖ Search yourself, answer hard questions and confront those areas that would hinder you from reaching your destination.
- ❖ Allow God to breathe new life into your purpose and destiny.
- ❖ Make sure you journal your experiences.

Table of Contents

1 - Destiny Is Calling You   8

2 - Destiny Matters   19

3 - Destiny Requires Faith   27

4 - Destiny Requires Courage   34

5 - Destiny At Times Will Require Letting Go   41

6 - Destiny Requires Forgiveness   50

7 - Destiny Requires Moving Beyond Your Comfort Zone 57

8 - Destiny In Motion *- Final Words*   65

1

DESTINY IS CALLING YOU

But by the grace of God I am what I am, and his grace toward me was not in vain. On the contrary, I worked harder than any of them, though it was not I, but the grace of God that is with me.
1 Corinthians 15:10

Destiny Brought to Life

In order to know that destiny is calling you, you first must accept the fact that God has given you one. Our God has created and fashioned you with specificity for a certain call. This call will require more than your "yes." You must then move out and do what has been instructed in order that the assignment is completed. Life has a way of making us feel as if we do not have anything to offer, or that we have messed up so badly that there is no way that He could ever use us. Well, let me help you today! We serve a God that specializes in people that have messed up; people that have been frowned upon;

people that have been counted out, pushed aside and made to feel less valuable than others. If you do not believe me, take a look at this list of people who were thought to be unworthy, unfit and not good enough according to society and their family members.

Adam
The first man; was a blame shifter who couldn't resist peer pressure. *(Genesis 3:12)*

Eve
The first woman; could not control her appetite and, should we say, had the first eating disorder? *(Genesis 3:6)*

Cain
The firstborn human being who murdered his brother. *(Genesis 4:8)*

Noah
The last righteous man on earth at the time; he was a drunk who slept in the nude. *(Genesis 9:20-21)*

Abraham
The forefather of faith; let other men walk off with his wife on two different occasions. *(Genesis 12 and 20)*

Sarah

The most gorgeous woman by popular opinion; let her husband sleep with another woman and then hated her for it. *(Genesis 16)*

Lot

Lost his father early in life and had a serious problem with choosing the wrong company. *(Genesis 18-20)*

Job

Supposedly a contemporary of Abraham and the epitome of faith; who suffered from the nagging of a faithless wife. *(Job 2:9)*

Isaac

Was nearly killed by his father; talked his wife into concealing their marriage. *(Genesis 26)*

Rebekah

The first "mail order bride," who turned out to be a rather manipulative wife. *(Genesis 27)*

Jacob

Out-wrestled God and was basically a pathological deceiver. *(Genesis 25, 27, 30)*

Rachel

Wrote the book on love at first sight; was a nomadic kleptomaniac. *(Genesis 31:19)*

Reuben

The pride and firstborn of Jacob; was a pervert who slept with his father's concubine. *(Genesis 35:21)*

Moses

The humblest man on the face of the earth *(Numbers 12:13)* had a very serious problem with his temper. *(Exodus 2, 32:19; Numbers 20:11)*

Aaron

Watched Jehovah triumph over Pharaoh; formed an abominable idol during an apparent episode of attention deficit disorder or perhaps colossal amnesia. *(Exodus 32)*

Miriam

The songwriter, had sibling jealousy and a greed for power. *(Numbers 12)*

Samson

Put Arnold Schwarzenegger and Jesse Ventura to shame; was hopelessly enmeshed with a disloyal wife—and ended up taking his own life. *(Judges 16)*

David

David dealt with lust and a lack of self-discipline *(2 Samuel 11:1-26)*

The Woman Caught in the Act of Adultery

The men wanted to kill her, but Jesus turned and showed her loving kindness and instructed her: "Neither do I condemn you. Go and sin no more" and used her story as a testimony until this very day. *(John 8)*

Peter

His issue was pride. *(Matthew 26:31-35, 69-75)*

The Woman at the Well

She had five husbands and was living with the sixth. *(John 4)*

Paul

Known for killing thousands of Christians, only to become one of the greatest Apostles of the New Testament.

Did you see that? God wants you to notice that from these lives that it does not matter what you have done. His desire to use you really has nothing to do with you! It has nothing to do with the mistakes that you have made, because it's not you, but it's HIM living on the inside of you. Before God created you, He called you; and in that call He already knew the mistakes that you would make. He knew the challenges that you would face, and even so, He *still* called you. It is in this season that He is calling for an even greater understanding of who you are in Him; and the fact that if there is breath in your body, God has need of you. I need you to understand that there are people that are assigned to you, who are literally waiting on you. They cannot come out of darkness into His light, until you get in position to bring them out by the grace of God. All God is waiting on is for you to answer His call to destiny. Just because you have picked up this book, I believe you are ready!

Let's go.....

Your Destiny Challenge
Ask God the Hard Questions

1. You may ask questions such as:
   a. God, what have You called me to do?

   _____

   _____

   _____

   b. Is this me or is this really You, God?

   _____

   _____

   _____

c. How will I know for sure?

_____

_____

_____

Confirmation is not a bad thing when it comes to understanding your destiny. You must be certain about what you have heard.

2. Write the vision that God shows you for your life plainly.

_____

_____

_____

_____

_____

3. Commit to accomplishing it until you see it manifest before your eyes and everyone else's as well.

_____

_____

_____

_____

_____

4. Ask God to show you and confirm your assignment in the earth.

_____

_____

_____

_____

_____

_____

_____

_____

- ❖ **WRITE, WRITE, WRITE** your journey.
- ❖ Keep vision casting and forecasting.
- ❖ Commit to completing your assignments until you accomplish them.

Destiny Moments of Meditation

For the vision is yet for an appointed time, but at the end it shall speak, and not lie: though it tarry, wait for it; because it will surely come, it will not tarry. (*Habakkuk 2:3 KJV*)

The Lord will fulfill his purpose for me; your steadfast love, O Lord, endures forever. Do not forsake the work of your hands. (*Psalm 138:8 ESV*)

I have said these things to you, that in me you may have peace. In the world you will have tribulation. But take heart; I have overcome the world. (*John 16:33 ESV*)

So shall my word be that goeth forth out of my mouth: it shall not return unto me void, but it shall accomplish that which I please, and it shall prosper in the thing whereto I sent it. (*Isaiah 55:11 KJV*)

We know that all things work together for good to those who love God, to those who are called according to His purpose. For those whom he foreknew he also predestined to be conformed to the image of his Son, in order that he might be the firstborn among many brothers. (*Romans 8:28-29)*

Commit your work to the Lord, and your plans will be established. (*Proverbs 16:3 ESV)*

All Scripture is breathed out by God and profitable for teaching, for reproof, for correction, and for training in righteousness. (*2 Timothy 3:16 ESV)*

For we are his workmanship, created in Christ Jesus for good works, which God prepared beforehand, that we should walk in them. (*Ephesians 2:10 ESV)*

Little children, you are from God and have overcome them, for he who is in you is greater than he who is in the world.
(*1 John 4:4 ESV)*

Chronicles of Destiny Workbook

Chronicle Your Own Destiny by Writing Your Journey

Chronicle Your Own Destiny by Writing Your Journey

2

DESTINY MATTERS

For I know the thoughts and plans that I have for you, says the Lord, thoughts and plans for welfare and peace and not for evil, to give you hope in your final outcome.
Jeremiah 29:11 AMP

Destiny Brought to Life

On any given day you may ask different people where they think thoughts and plans originate from and in most instances you will get a variety of different answers. For many, society teaches them that thoughts and plans all start in the mind. That is true to a certain degree, but even then, they still have an originating source. Was it something that the individual heard, or saw? Was it something that they were missing in life? Did those thoughts come from a place of lack, or feelings of inadequacy? Regardless, the thoughts were formed from a source. However, when it comes to the thoughts and plans for a Believer, it is important to note that they all start in the mind of God.

He has always had a purpose and destiny in mind for you! I know that at times that can be hard to believe. No matter what you have done, or what it currently looks like, God can take your heartache and pain and use it to work towards achieving His plans and purposes in your life. He is such an amazing God that He causes it all to work together for your destiny to come into fruition (Romans 8:28). I know many that have looked at their mistakes and decided that it was over and they thought they could never reach their goals. Later, God sent someone to show them how those mistakes would actually equip, and fortify them to achieve all that He had planned from the beginning. Now, if you do not know God's thoughts toward you, then you will never know that your destiny matters and you will never understand that He has a plan for your life.

Oftentimes it may seem that as soon as we realize that we have a God-ordained destiny, the enemy sends everything our way to keep us from getting there. You must begin to look at what you are encountering differently. Understand that because you know God's plans and purposes for your life, your destiny does matter. So the tactics of the enemy could not possibly be working against you. Therefore, it must be working for you! Achieving destiny means that you must possess great confidence in your God and what He has placed inside of you. He will give you everything that you need to be all that He has called you to be.

Remember:

- ❖ Always give every thought and idea back to God.
- ❖ Challenge yourself to grow in your purpose and destiny daily.
- ❖ Pray for witty inventions and fresh revelation.

Your Destiny Challenge

1. Today ask God to reveal to you what His thoughts are towards you. Write them down. *They can be as simple as...God thinks that I am perfectly made; God thinks that I am made just like Him; God thinks that I am strong etc.*

2. Locate and research five (5) organizations or people that are doing what God has given you to do.

1._____

2._____

3._____

4._____

5._____

3. Write down challenges that you have faced, and ask Him to show you His hand in using those challenges to bring you to your expected end.

_____

_____

_____

_____

_____

_____

_____

_____

❖ Motivate yourself.
❖ Surround yourself with positive people.
❖ Build your character and be a person of integrity.

Destiny Moments of Meditation

Before I formed you in the womb I knew you; and before you were born I sanctified you, and I ordained you a prophet to the nations. (*Jeremiah 1:5 MEV*)

Hear counsel and receive instruction, that you may be wise in your latter days. (*Proverbs 19:20 MEV*)

But we speak the wisdom of God in a mystery, the hidden wisdom, which God ordained before the ages for our glory. None of the rulers of this age knew it. For had they known it, they would not have crucified the Lord of glory. But as it is written, Eye has not seen, nor ear heard, nor has it entered into the heart of man the things which God has prepared for those who love Him. (*1 Corinthians 2:7-9 MEV*)

By no means! Let God be true though everyone were a liar, as it is written, that you may be justified in your words, and prevail when you are judged. (*Romans 3:4 ESV*)

And let steadfastness have its full effect, that you may be perfect and complete, lacking in nothing. (*James 1:4*)

No weapon that is fashioned against you shall succeed, and you shall confute every tongue that rises against you in judgment. This is the heritage of the servants of the LORD and their vindication from me, declares the LORD. (*Isaiah 54:17 ESV*)

Declaring the end from the beginning, and from ancient times the things that are not yet done, saying, My counsel shall stand, and I will do all My good pleasure. (*Isaiah 46:10 MEV*)

Whatever happens, it has already been given a name, and it is known what man is; he cannot contend with Him who is stronger than he. (*Ecclesiastes 6:10 MEV*)

And a stone of stumbling, and a rock of offense. They stumble because they disobey the word, as they were destined to do. But you are a chosen race, a royal priesthood, a holy nation, a people for his own possession, that you may proclaim the excellencies of him who called you out of darkness into his marvelous light. (*1 Peter 2:8-9 ESV*)

A man's steps are from the Lord; how then can man understand his way? (*Proverbs 20:24 ESV*)

Chronicle Your Own Destiny by Writing Your Journey

Chronicle Your Own Destiny by Writing Your Journey

3

DESTINY REQUIRES FAITH

For we walk by faith, not by sight.
2 Corinthians 5:7

Destiny Brought to Life

One thing is for certain, when God sent Jesus into the earth, He had a specific purpose in mind for His life, just as He does for you and me. He created us with specificity, with a purpose, a destiny, and a plan in mind. From the beginning of time, it has been the enemy's plan to cause each of us to deviate from that plan, and thus thwarting the perfect will of God for our lives. With all that is going on in the world, it takes faith to believe that God still has a desire to use many of us. However, it is faith that will cause us to look beyond our present day circumstances and look to Him, because He is the Author and the Finisher of our faith and will cause us to get to our expected end. The enemy of this world still tries to discourage us, trap us, and lie to and on us. He still desires to cause us to view ourselves as defeated as we face day to day challenges.

God has given each of us a task to complete in the earth and we cannot do it without Him. God desires for us to constantly walk by faith and not by sight and it will take various degrees of faith to reach our destiny. The prophetic works two ways. First, we hear what God desires for us to have, accomplish, and obtain, then we must activate our faith in order to do such. God will help us to accomplish all that He has set before us; even miracles will not take place unless we exercise our faith. It is your faith that will cause chains to break; your faith is what will cause walls, obstacles, and giants to come down! It is your faith that will cause sick bodies to be healed. It is your faith that will cause you to continue to press on when others seem to have dropped out of the race. Soaring in faith requires you to always remember that you were chosen for this assignment. So you must act like it at all times, regardless to what it looks like. The only way to do that is to always soar with eagles and leave the chickens on the ground where they belong! Remember, everyone is not ordained to go with you. Either they will charge and challenge your faith and cause you to soar higher, or they will drain you of your faith and ultimately cause you to remain in a low place. The decision is yours. I challenge you to move toward Destiny today and continue to Blaze Forward!

<u>Your Destiny Challenge</u>
Put your faith in action. Begin to challenge your faith.

1. Write down 3 relatively easy things that you believe God for. I chose the number three because this is a holy journey that you are on and it will require the covering of the Father, the sacrifices of the Son, and the leading and guiding of the Holy Spirit to be with you.

     1._____

     2._____

     3._____

2. Write down 2 hard things that you are believing God for. I chose the number 2 because you need to know that God is in agreement with you; and He is all you need in order to see what He ordained to come to pass.

     1._____

     2._____

Remember:

❖ Encourage yourself.
❖ Be persistent.
❖ Mentor those of likeminded faith.

Destiny Moments of Meditation

I have been crucified with Christ. It is no longer I who live, but Christ who lives in me. And the life I now live in the flesh, I live by faith in the Son of God, [a] who loved me and gave Himself for me. (*Galatians 2:20 MEV*)

But let him ask in faith, without wavering. For he who wavers is like a wave of the sea, driven and tossed with the wind. (*James 1:6 MEV*)

He who believes in Me, as the Scripture has said, out of his heart shall flow rivers of living water. (*John 7:38 MEV*)

Jesus said to him, Go your way. Your faith has made you well. Immediately he received his sight and followed Jesus on the way. (*Mark 10:52 MEV*)

Therefore I say to you, whatever things you ask when you pray, believe that you will receive them, and you will have them. (*Mark 11:24 MEV*)

Do not be conformed to this world, but be transformed by the renewing of your mind, that you may prove what is the good and acceptable and perfect will of God. (*Romans 12:2 MEV*)

Thus says the LORD, who makes a way in the sea, a path in the mighty waters, who brings forth chariot and horse, army and warrior; they lie down, they cannot rise, they are extinguished, quenched like a wick: "Remember not the former things, nor consider the things of old. Behold, I am doing a new thing; now it springs forth, do you not perceive it? I will make a way in the wilderness and rivers in the desert. *(Isaiah 43:16-19 ESV)*

Now faith is the substance of things hoped for, the evidence of things not seen. *Hebrews (11:1 KJV)*

Brothers, I do not consider that I have made it my own. But one thing I do: forgetting what lies behind and straining forward to what lies ahead *(Philippians 3:13 ESV)*

For the Father loves the Son and shows him all that he himself is doing. And greater works than these will he show him, so that you may marvel. *(John 5:20 ESV)*

Chronicles of Destiny Workbook

Chronicle Your Own Destiny by Writing Your Journey

_____

_____

_____

_____

_____

_____

_____

_____

_____

_____

_____

_____

_____

_____

_____

_____

_____

_____

_____

_____

_____

_____

_____

_____

_____

_____

4

DESTINY REQUIRES COURAGE

Be strong and courageous, for you shall provide the land that I swore to their fathers to give them as an inheritance for this people. Be strong and very courageous, in order to act carefully in accordance with all the law that My servant Moses commanded you. Do not turn aside from it to the right or the left, so that you may succeed wherever you go. This Book of the Law must not depart from your mouth. Meditate on it day and night so that you may act carefully according to all that is written in it. For then you will make your way successful, and you will be wise. Have not I commanded you? Be strong and courageous. Do not be afraid or dismayed, for the LORD your God is with you wherever you go.
Joshua 1:6-9 MEV

Destiny Brought to Life

Courage is defined as bravery. It is the choice and willingness to confront agony, pain, uncertainty, or intimidation; the quality of mind or spirit that enables a person to face difficulty and danger without fear. So, the basic meaning of courage is to do something beyond your fears. Destiny has its own set of fears that each individual must overcome. The good news is that we can all overcome them. Joshua's story reminds us to be strong in the Lord and courageous for His Kingdom. Courage requires strength. It takes strength to face your fears and to accept the realization that a place has gotten too small for you. It takes strength to accept the fact that the people that you grew up with are going another direction and be OK with it. God used the life of Joshua to teach us many lessons today. Joshua knew how to lead, but before leading, he learned the art of following. He served Moses until the day he died, yet he still had to resist the urge to stay in the place of mourning over his beloved leader. So, God uses Joshua's life to teach us to have the courage to let go of dead things. There are some things that are unproductive and that discredit the Kingdom of God. Yes, Joshua teaches us to have the courage to walk away, even when we still love them! Selah!

Joshua also teaches us how to have courage and to be fearless in the things of God. We can rely on God because He is the One that knows the end from the beginning. Courage has a lot to do with who and where we choose to reside. I am not just talking physically, but mentally as well. We must connect with courageous people, who are influential and challenge us to go to the next dimension. If you are going to be courageous, you simply must learn how to work your God-given sphere of influence. Understand that courage does not come from us, but is indeed a gift from our Father in heaven. Take some time today and ask God to increase, not just your faith, but your courage as well and watch Him move on your behalf.

Your Destiny Challenge

1. Refresh your mind often with what God said.
2. Were there any changes or additions? If so, add it plainly to your life vision.
3. Write down 3 things that you will do this week to move towards what He has said.

     1._____

     2._____

     3._____

4. List 4 ways that you will motivate yourself to move into your destiny and then do them.

     1._____

     2._____

     3._____

     4._____

Remember:

❖ Put on the mind of Christ.
❖ Learn to forget what is behind; reach forward and press for the prize ahead.

❖ Release the baggage, (yours and others) it only slows and holds you down.

Destiny Moments of Meditation

Be strong and courageous. Do not fear or be in dread of them, for it is the Lord your God who goes with you. He will not leave you or forsake you." (*Deuteronomy 31:6 ESV*)

For God gave us a spirit not of fear but of power and love and self-control. (*2 Timothy 1:7 ESV*)

The wicked flee when no man pursueth: but the righteous are bold as a lion. (*Proverbs 28:1 KJV*)

Trust in the Lord with all your heart, and do not lean on your own understanding. In all your ways acknowledge him, and he will make straight your paths. (*Proverbs 3:5-6 ESV*)

Then David said to Solomon his son, "Be strong and courageous and do it. Do not be afraid and do not be dismayed, for the Lord God, even my God, is with you. He will not leave you or forsake you, until all the work for the service of the house of the Lord is finished. (*1 Chronicles 28:20 ESV*)

I can do all things through him who strengthens me. (*Philippians 4:13 ESV*)

No temptation has overtaken you that are not common to man. God is faithful, and he will not let you be tempted beyond your ability, but with the temptation he will also provide the way of escape, that you may be able to endure it. (*1 Corinthians 10:13 ESV*)

And Jesus said to him, "If you can'! All things are possible for one who believes." (*Mark 9:23 ESV*)

For whoever would save his life will lose it, but whoever loses his life for my sake will find it. (*Matthew 16:25 ESV*)

Again I saw that under the sun the race is not to the swift, nor the battle to the strong, nor bread to the wise, nor riches to the intelligent, nor favor to those with knowledge, but time and chance happen to them all. (*Ecclesiastes 9:11 ESV*)

_____

_____

_____

_____

_____

_____

_____

_____

_____

_____

_____

_____

_____

_____

_____

_____

_____

_____

_____

_____

_____

_____

_____

_____

_____

_____

_____

_____

Chronicle Your Own Destiny by Writing Your Journey

_____

_____

_____

_____

_____

_____

_____

_____

_____

_____

_____

_____

_____

_____

_____

_____

_____

_____

_____

_____

_____

_____

_____

_____

_____

_____

_____

5

DESTINY REQUIRES LETTING GO

I am the true vine, and my Father is the gardener. He cuts off every branch in me that bears no fruit, while every branch that does bear fruit he prunes so that it will be even more fruitful. You are already clean because of the word I have spoken to you. Remain in me, as I also remain in you. No branch can bear fruit by itself; it must remain in the vine. Neither can you bear fruit unless you remain in me. I am the vine; you are the branches. If you remain in me and I in you, you will bear much fruit; apart from me you can do nothing. If you do not remain in me, you are like a branch that is thrown away and withers; such branches are picked up, thrown into the fire and burned. If you remain in me and my words remain in you, ask whatever you wish, and it will be done for you. This is to my Father's glory, that you bear much fruit, showing yourselves to be my disciples.
John 15:1-8

Destiny Brought to Life

I must admit, I am not very good when it comes to growing plants, although my mother has "green thumb." As a young girl, I would watch closely as she would take one plant from one pot and transplant it into a larger one. Simply because the pot was too small and there was not enough room to promote healthy growth. I have seen her cut branches and pull dead leaves from plants season after season. There were many days that I would sit there and wonder why she was cutting the plant when she should be trying to get it to grow. Listen, there are times and seasons in our lives where God requires us to cut things and sometimes people out of our lives. We may not see the necessary point in cutting back or releasing them, but in the infinite wisdom of God, He sees and knows what is best for each of us.

Letting things and people go does not necessarily mean that there was a rift, tear, or even "a falling out." Most times it simply means that we have gone as far as we can go in this season of our journey. In order for us both to reach our full potential in destiny, we simply must go our separate ways. Sometimes it is because we have learned and depended on others far too much. At other times, without realizing it, we have put others in a place that was designed for God and God alone. Before the foundations of the world, God took each of us and He grafted us into His vine, which is Christ Jesus, our Lord. It is in that Vine that we have the sources of the nutrients that we need. He causes everything to work in and through us, and ultimately, He is the One that causes fruit to be produced out of us. In order for the best fruit to be produced, there will be times of pruning, cutting, and even times of digging.

As we travel on the road to destiny, there are times that weeds begin to grow, and will choke our very existence away, unless the gardener notices and gets to them first. It is when the *Good Gardener* notices that the weeds are trying to take us away from the divine plan of God, that He will call for a breaking away. During those times we must trust Him as never before, because He knows what is best for us. When God is moving, you have no choice but to move! Trust Him today!

Your Destiny Challenge

1. Over the next several days take a few moments each day and sit quietly. Ask God to reveal to you things that you have held on to that He is really calling for you to release.

   _____

   _____

   _____

   _____

   _____

   _____

   _____

2. Write them down. Do not stop writing them until you feel that He is finished speaking. For many, this will not be easy, but it is necessary for your destiny to unfold.

_____

_____

_____

_____

_____

_____

_____

_____

_____

_____

3. Once you have your list, pray and ask God to show you how to release them. Most times you won't have to do anything. However, if He shows you specific things that you must do, I challenge you to move with the timing of the Lord and do them as He has instructed. The season of cutting back and pruning will be as a child that wore one pair of shoes at the end of the school year, only to need a new pair when the new school year begins. Not because if is fashionable, but because you have hit a growth spurt over the summer and what once fit, simply does not fit any longer!

Remember:
- ❖ Be an influencer, an exhorter, an encourager… the results will be Divine.
- ❖ Complete your assignments.
- ❖ Pray daily for Divine guidance.

Destiny Moments of Meditation

I the LORD search the heart and test the mind, to give every man according to his ways, according to the fruit of his deeds. (*Jeremiah 17:10 EVS*)

God is not man, that he should lie, or a son of man, that he should change his mind. (*Numbers 23:19 ESV*)

For by grace you have been saved through faith. And this is not your own doing; it is the gift of God, not a result of works, so that no one may boast. (*Ephesians 2:8-9 ESV*)

For many, of whom I have often told you and now tell you even with tears, walk as enemies of the cross of Christ. Their end is destruction, their god is their belly, and they glory in their shame, with minds set on earthly things. But our citizenship is in heaven, and from it we await a Savior, the Lord Jesus Christ, who will transform our lowly body to be like his glorious body. (*Philippians 3:18-20 ESV*)

You see that a person is justified by works and not by faith alone. *(James 2:24)*

For he will complete what he appoints for me, and many such things are in his mind. *(Job 23:14 ESV)*

Jesus replied, "A man was going down from Jerusalem to Jericho, and he fell among robbers, who stripped him and beat him and departed, leaving him half dead. Now by chance a priest was going down that road, and when he saw him he passed by on the other side. So likewise a Levite, when he came to the place and saw him, passed by on the other side. But a Samaritan, as he journeyed, came to where he was, and when he saw him, he had compassion. He went to him and bound up his wounds, pouring on oil and wine. Then he set him on his own animal and brought him to an inn and took care of him. *(Luke 10:30-37 ESV)*

Religion that is pure and undefiled before God, the Father, is this: to visit orphans and widows in their affliction, and to keep oneself unstained from the world. *(James 1:27 ESV)*

By faith Noah, being warned by God concerning events as yet unseen, in reverent fear constructed an ark for the saving of his household. By this he condemned the world and became an heir of the righteousness that comes by faith. *(Hebrews 11:7 ESV)*

I call heaven and earth to witness against you today, that I have set before you life and death, blessing and curse. Therefore choose life, that you and your offspring may live. (*Deuteronomy 30:19 ESV*)

Chronicle Your Own Destiny by Writing Your Journey

_____

_____

_____

_____

_____

_____

_____

_____

_____

_____

_____

_____

_____

_____

_____

_____

_____

_____

_____

_____

_____

_____

_____

_____

_____

_____

_____

_____

_____

6

DESTINY REQUIRES FORGIVENESS

*Then came Peter to him, and said, Lord, how oft shall my brother sin against me,
and I forgive him? Till seven times? Jesus saith unto him, I say not unto thee,
Until seven times: but, Until seventy times seven.*
Matthew 18:21-22

Destiny Brought to Life

When it comes to forgiving others, Jesus was rather clear on the issue. Yet, it still seems to be an issue that we struggle with. You will never get to your future holding on to things of the past. I get it; forgiveness can be one of the hardest things to do! Yet, so is destiny! Destiny is hard enough to achieve without carrying the baggage of unforgiveness along with it.

The enemy uses unforgiveness as a way to bind us to our past, when God has clearly called us into our future! Unforgiveness will hold you hostage, while forgiveness is crying out, "I've come to set you free." Walking in total forgiveness is a choice. When you choose to let go, and walk in the forgiveness that our Father extends to us on a daily basis, it will cause you to realize that God has a way of using it all for your good. Perhaps this person's season is up in your life. Maybe, just maybe God allowed this to happen to work patience, forgiveness or to give you the opportunity to show the love of God to someone that may not deserve it. When people do things to you, seek to understand what the real lesson is and realize that some people are not meant to be a part of your future. After all, your assignment is too great for you to hold on to anything that is not a part of it! So learn today to release it and let it go, and do it quickly for destiny's sake!

Your Destiny Challenge

1. Make a list of those that may have disappointed, rejected, broke your trust, did not meet your expectations or abandoned you. This list can be as long as you need it to be. Do not rush it. You will know when God is finished breathing on it, because the weight, or the heaviness in your sprit will lift. Be totally honest with God and with yourself! This is not the season to hold anything back. Thank God today for giving you a time and space in the

privacy of your favorite secret place to get it all out! You cannot allow anything to get in the way of your destiny. Therefore, forgiveness is absolutely necessary; and not just once or twice either....You read the scripture *until seventy times seven* (Matthew 18:22). That's a place of unlimited forgiveness. Release it today, because there will come a time that you too will need forgiveness.

_____

_____

_____

_____

_____

_____

_____

_____

Remember:
- ❖ Diligently serve those you are called too.
- ❖ Aim high but remain humble.
- ❖ Be intentional.

Destiny Moments of Meditation

Jesus said to them, "My food is to do the will of him who sent me and to accomplish his work. (*John 4:34 ESV*)

For you formed my inward parts; you knitted me together in my mother's womb. I praise you, for I am fearfully and wonderfully made. Wonderful are your works; my soul knows it very well. My frame was not hidden from you, when I was being made in secret, intricately woven in the depths of the earth. Your eyes saw my unformed substance; in your book were written, every one of them, the days that were formed for me, when as yet there was none of them. (*Psalm 139:13-16 ESV*)

And he saw that they were making headway painfully, for the wind was against them. And about the fourth watch of the night he came to them, walking on the sea. He meant to pass by them. (*Mark 6:48 ESV*)

Blessed is the man who walks not in the counsel of the wicked, nor stands in the way of sinners, nor sits in the seat of scoffers; but his delight is in the law of the LORD, and on his law he meditates day and night. He is like a tree planted by streams of water that yields its fruit in its season, and its leaf does not wither. In all that he does, he prospers. The wicked are not so, but are like chaff that the wind drives away. Therefore the wicked will not stand in the judgment, nor sinners in the congregation of the righteous; (*Psalm 1:1-6 ESV*)

Therefore, brothers, be all the more diligent to make your calling and election sure, for if you practice these qualities you will never fall. For in this way there will be richly provided for you an entrance into the eternal kingdom of our Lord and Savior Jesus Christ. (*2 Peter 1:10-11 ESV*)

But someone will say, "You have faith and I have works." Show me your faith apart from your works, and I will show you my faith by my works. (*James 2:18 ESV*)

Rejoice always. (*1 Thessalonians 5:16 ESV*)

We must not indulge in sexual immorality as some of them did, and twenty-three thousand fell in a single day. (*1 Corinthians 10:8 ESV*)

For the gifts and the calling of God are irrevocable. (*Romans 11:29 ESV*)

And those whom he predestined he also called, and those whom he called he also justified, and those whom he justified he also glorified. (*Romans 8:30 ESV*)

Chronicle Your Own Destiny by Writing Your Journey

_____

_____

_____

_____

_____

_____

_____

_____

_____

_____

_____

_____

_____

_____

_____

_____

_____

_____

_____

_____

_____

_____

_____

_____

_____

_____

_____

Chronicle Your Own Destiny by Writing Your Journey

_____

_____

_____

_____

_____

_____

_____

_____

_____

_____

_____

_____

_____

_____

_____

_____

_____

_____

_____

_____

_____

_____

_____

_____

7

DESTINY REQUIRES MOVING OUT OF YOUR COMFORT ZONE

The LORD had said to Abram, "Go from your country, your people and your father's household to the land I will show you.
Genesis 12:1 KJV

Destiny Brought to Life

When Destiny landed at Abram's doorstep, it came with an immediate assignment. God commanded him to leave his father's house and go to a place where he had never been before. I have been in this season of life a time or two and it is a place like no other. Leaving the comforts of daddy's house will challenge everything about you because it is a place of uncertainty. There are times that discontentment will sit in your very soul and cause you to wonder if you truly heard the voice of the Lord. Leaving daddy's house will sometimes cause you to step out only on a word from the Lord. Since we are made in His image, we should not be surprised when He calls us to step out. After all, He stepped out into nothing but darkness and said, "Let there be," and there was.

As people of destiny, we must be careful not to become stagnate and stuck in a familiar place. Staying in a place longer than what God has said will cause your anointing to become dull. Your destiny is far too great to be stuck in a place beyond your expiration date! You will never know what the outcome of will be unless you make a decision to trust God completely and go wherever He leads you. Staying too long will cause fear to overtake you, and contentment to grab a greater hold on you day by day.

Our God did not give us the spirit of fear, but He gave us power, love and a sound mind. All of the amazing things that you saw yourself accomplishing in the spirit; everything that you ever hoped for, ever wanted or desired can literally be one decision outside of your comfort zone. As God unction's you to move forward places that He has yet to show you, there will be days that you will learn to do as David did and encourage yourself in the Lord! Fear not, He is right there with you. Too many are waiting on you for you to remain stuck.

<u>Your Destiny Challenge</u>

1. Write a list of five (5) things that you are uncomfortable doing or you never thought you'd ever do.

    1._____

    2._____

    3._____

    4._____

    5._____

2. Now pick three (3) and do them. *Do not move to the next Moment in Destiny until you do!*

    1. _____

    2. _____

    3. _____

Once completed, you should have a new sense of liberation and confidence. Why? Because you literally did what the enemy said that you would never do! Now that you have pushed through some uncomfortable things, go on and explore a whole new world that God wants to open your eyes to!

Remember:
- ❖ Faithfulness produces fruitfulness.
- ❖ Refresh your mind with what God said about you.
- ❖ Pray over your purpose and destiny daily.

Destiny Moments of Meditation

And while he was at Bethany in the house of Simon the leper, as he was reclining at table, a woman came with an alabaster flask of ointment of pure nard, very costly, and she broke the flask and poured it over his head. There were some who said to themselves indignantly, "Why was the ointment wasted like that? For this ointment could have been sold for more than three hundred denarii and given to the poor." And they scolded her. But Jesus said, "Leave her alone. Why do you trouble her? She has done a beautiful thing to me. For you always have the poor with you, and whenever you want, you can do good for them. But you will not always have me. (*Mark 14:3-10 ESV*)

And he said to them, "To you has been given the secret of the kingdom of God, but for those outside everything is in parables (*Mark 4:11 ESV*)

Not everyone who says to me, 'Lord, Lord,' will enter the kingdom of heaven, but the one who does the will of my Father who is in heaven. On that day many will say to me, 'Lord, Lord, did we not prophesy in your name, and cast out demons in your name, and do many mighty works in your name?' And then will I declare to them, 'I never knew you; depart from me, you workers of lawlessness. (*Matthew 7:21-23 ESV*)

Give ear to my prayer, O God, and hide not yourself from my plea for mercy! Attend to me, and answer me; I am restless in my complaint and I moan, because of the noise of the enemy, because of the oppression of the wicked. For they drop trouble upon me, and in anger they bear a grudge against me. My heart is in anguish within me; the terrors of death have fallen upon me. Fear and trembling come upon me, and horror overwhelms me. (*Psalm 55:1-23 ESV*)

I know that you can do all things, and that no purpose of yours can be thwarted. (*Job 42:2 ESV*)

In him we have obtained an inheritance, having been predestined according to the purpose of him who works all things according to the counsel of his will (*Ephesians 1:11 ESV*)

And now I commend you to God and to the word of his grace, which is able to build you up and to give you the inheritance among all those who are sanctified. (*Acts 20:32 ESV*)

The word of the LORD that came to Hosea, the son of Beeri, in the days of Uzziah, Jotham, Ahaz, and Hezekiah, kings of Judah and in the days of Jeroboam the son of Joash, king of

Israel. When the LORD first spoke through Hosea, the LORD said to Hosea, "Go, take to yourself a wife of whoredom and have children of whoredom, for the land commits great whoredom by forsaking the LORD." So he went and took Gomer, the daughter of Diblaim, and she conceived and bore him a son. And the LORD said to him, "Call his name Jezreel, for in just a little while I will punish the house of Jehu for the blood of Jezreel, and I will put an end to the kingdom of the house of Israel. And on that day I will break the bow of Israel in the Valley of Jezreel. (*Hosea 1:1-11 ESV*)

You are my hammer and weapon of war: with you I break nations in pieces; with you I destroy kingdoms; with you I break in pieces the horse and his rider; with you I break in pieces the chariot and the charioteer; with you I break in pieces man and woman; with you I break in pieces the old man and the youth; with you I break in pieces the young man and the young woman; with you I break in pieces the shepherd and his flock; with you I break in pieces the farmer and his team; with you I break in pieces governors and commanders. (*Jeremiah 51:20-23 ESV*)

Who desires all people to be saved and to come to the knowledge of the truth. (*1 Timothy 2:4 ESV*)

Chronicles of Destiny Workbook

Chronicle Your Own Destiny by Writing Your Journey

_____

_____

_____

_____

_____

_____

_____

_____

_____

_____

_____

_____

_____

_____

_____

_____

_____

_____

_____

_____

_____

_____

_____

_____

_____

_____

_____

8

Final Words
DESTINY IN MOTION

As a final thought, I want to remind you that destiny unfolds day by day. However, if you never trust God, and not just shift, but obey during times and seasons that He instructs you to, you will never obtain it. God does not just want you to obey, but He wants you to do it quickly. It is imperative that you learn to do it now, because the harder tasks are coming. Remember when God instructed Abraham to take his son of promise to the mountains to slay him? If that is not hard, I do not know what is.

Obedience plays an intricate part in achieving it destiny. There is no place for disobedience. Obeying is not always easy, but it is possible. Reaching your purpose and destiny means that you must become as a sharp-shooter in the spirit and stay focused on your assignment! Yes, there will be people that will simply pass thru and then move on. However, do not get stuck on those that choose to move on. Learn to discern quickly why God has allowed certain people to come into your life. Once you discern why they are there, ensure that you complete the assignment given by God for their lives. Never focus on what you do not have or who left, and why. You simply must focus on what you have left. I have come to realize that leftovers are not always a bad thing. Leftovers are those things which remain. So, you see, we must learn to thank God for the leftovers and continue to press on toward the goal for the prize of the upward call of God in Christ Jesus (Philippians 3:14). Pressing forward requires strength and tenacity. It will require you to take a look at what is left in your hands and work it to the glory of God!

Stay passionate about what God has given you to do; and as you stay passionate others will too. You cannot afford to become comfortable and lose your fire because comfort is a destiny killer and too many people are counting on you fulfilling the call of God on your life. However, as you begin to look over the possibilities of what today can bring, the Lord wants you to know that you must stick to His eternal plan. Never be afraid to allow Him to breathe on it again, to ensure that you get to your expected end because He is the Master

Build, and it is His plan, not ours. When things hit you unexpectedly, you can be encouraged knowing that there isn't anything that takes God by surprise, not even our own slip-ups or mishaps. He is The Master Planner and Master Builder, building something amazing out of your life's experiences. It doesn't matter who turns on you, who walks away, or who doesn't believe in you, God still has a plan for your life and your destiny matters. No matter what comes your way, learn to stay focused. Your focus will become your greatest weapon of warfare.

Face it, people will come and they will go. I once heard Apostle Eckhardt say that he has learned to try his best to live by the scripture that says, *If it be possible, as much as lieth in you, live peaceably with all men (Romans 12:18 KJV).* Now, trust me, our God knows that there will be some that we just are not able to live peaceably with, but we are to at least try. Purpose and destiny are too tedious to be distracted by envy, strife, and division; therefore you must pursue peace at all cost. Remain confident and consistent while you are fulfilling your assignment in the earth. There is no need for arrogance, but keep looking to the hills from whence comes your help; knowing that your help comes from the Lord, who made heaven and earth.

Trying times will not last always and He will not suffer your foot to be moved. Just as He continues to keep Israel, He is also keeping you! Be confident as you remember always that your self-worth or self-esteem does not come from people, but are locked into a greater system, called the Kingdom of Heaven.

Lastly, I want you to know that there will be times and seasons that it will seem as though no one around you will expect you to make it. There will be days and nights that you will seem all alone. It is then that you must remember that there are witnesses who surround us like clouds (Romans 12:1) and they will forever cheer both you and I on to the finish line. It will be these very witnesses that will literally catapult you into the next dimension of your purpose & destiny. As you go from glory to glory, accomplishing your assignment in the earth you will look back and know that it was truly the Lord's doing and there is no way that you can turn back now. Do you know why? Because it is your *due season*! Destiny is literally calling your name; can't you hear it? I know you can, and I am so grateful that you have answered the call. The Lord truly has need of you and so does the Body of Christ. It is time for you to ARISE to the next dimension of the call.

<u>Your Destiny Challenge</u>

1. Earlier you were asked to identify organizations that were a model for what God has created you to accomplish in the earth. Now, I want to challenge you to contact at least two of those organizations and ask if they

are willing to Mentor you and allow you to glean from them. If they say no, this is not the right time. Keep pressing until you locate someone to assist you. Do not get discouraged. Ask God to lead and direct you to the right person or place and He will properly connect you. We all need one another to get to the place called "there."

2. Seek out training and development opportunities to enhance what He has given you to accomplish.

Destiny Moments of Meditation

I can do all things through him who strengthens me. (*Philippians 4:13 ESV*)

For God gave us a spirit not of fear but of power and love and self-control. (*2 Timothy 1:7 ESV*)

Now faith is the assurance of things hoped for, the conviction of things not seen. For by it the people of old received their commendation. By faith we understand that the universe was created by the word of God, so that what is seen was not made out of things that are visible. By faith Abel offered to God a more acceptable sacrifice than Cain, through which he was commended as righteous, God commending him by accepting his gifts. And through his faith, though he died, he still speaks. By faith Enoch was taken up so that he should not see death, and he was not found, because God had taken him. Now before he was taken he was commended as having pleased God. (*Hebrews 11:1-40 ESV*)

For if you forgive others their trespasses, your heavenly Father will also forgive you, but if you do not forgive others their trespasses, neither will your Father forgive your trespasses. (*Matthew 6:14-15 ESV*)

Therefore, confess your sins to one another and pray for one another, that you may be healed. The prayer of a righteous person has great power as it is working. (*James 5:16 ESV*)

But I say to you who hear, Love your enemies, do good to those who hate you. (*Luke 6:27 ESV*)

For nothing will be impossible with God. (*Luke 1:37 ESV*)

For by grace you have been saved through faith. And this is not your own doing; it is the gift of God, not a result of works, so that no one may boast. (*Ephesians 2:8-9 ESV*)

Trust in the LORD with all your heart, and do not lean on your own understanding. In all your ways acknowledge him, and he will make straight your paths. (*Proverbs 3:5-6 ESV*)

The fear of the LORD is the beginning of knowledge, but fools despise wisdom and instruction. (*Proverbs 1:7 NIV*)

There is a way that appears to be right, but in the end it leads to death. (*Proverbs 14:12 NIV*)

Above all else, guard your heart, for everything you do flows from it. (*Proverbs 4:23 NIV*)

Every word of God is flawless; he is a shield to those who take refuge in him. (*Proverbs 30:5 NIV*)

Every word of God is pure: he is a shield unto them that put their trust in him. (*Proverbs 30:5 KJV*)

Iron sharpeneth iron; so a man sharpeneth the countenance of his friend. (*Proverbs 27:17 KJV*)

Where there is no revelation, people cast off restraint; but blessed are those who heed wisdom's instruction. (*Proverbs 29:18 NIV*)

Chronicle Your Own Destiny by Writing Your Journey

_____

_____

_____

_____

_____

_____

_____

_____

_____

_____

_____

_____

_____

_____

_____

_____

_____

_____

_____

_____

_____

_____

_____

_____

_____

_____

_____

_____

_____

Prophetess Tonya M. Parker

IN DUE SEASON
PubIishing